Customer Focus

Culture Change Series

Jim Peal, Ph.D.

LEADERSHIP
DEVELOPMENT GROUP

CUSTOMER FOCUS

BY

JAMES PEAL, PH.D

Published by
Leadership Development Group
Oakland CA USA
Tel. (01) 805-966-3323

Copyright 2014 by James Peal, Ph.D.

ISBN, 978-1500367657

First Printing 2014

Agreements

Engage and Participate

Confidentiality

Commit to make a difference

Insights Into Action

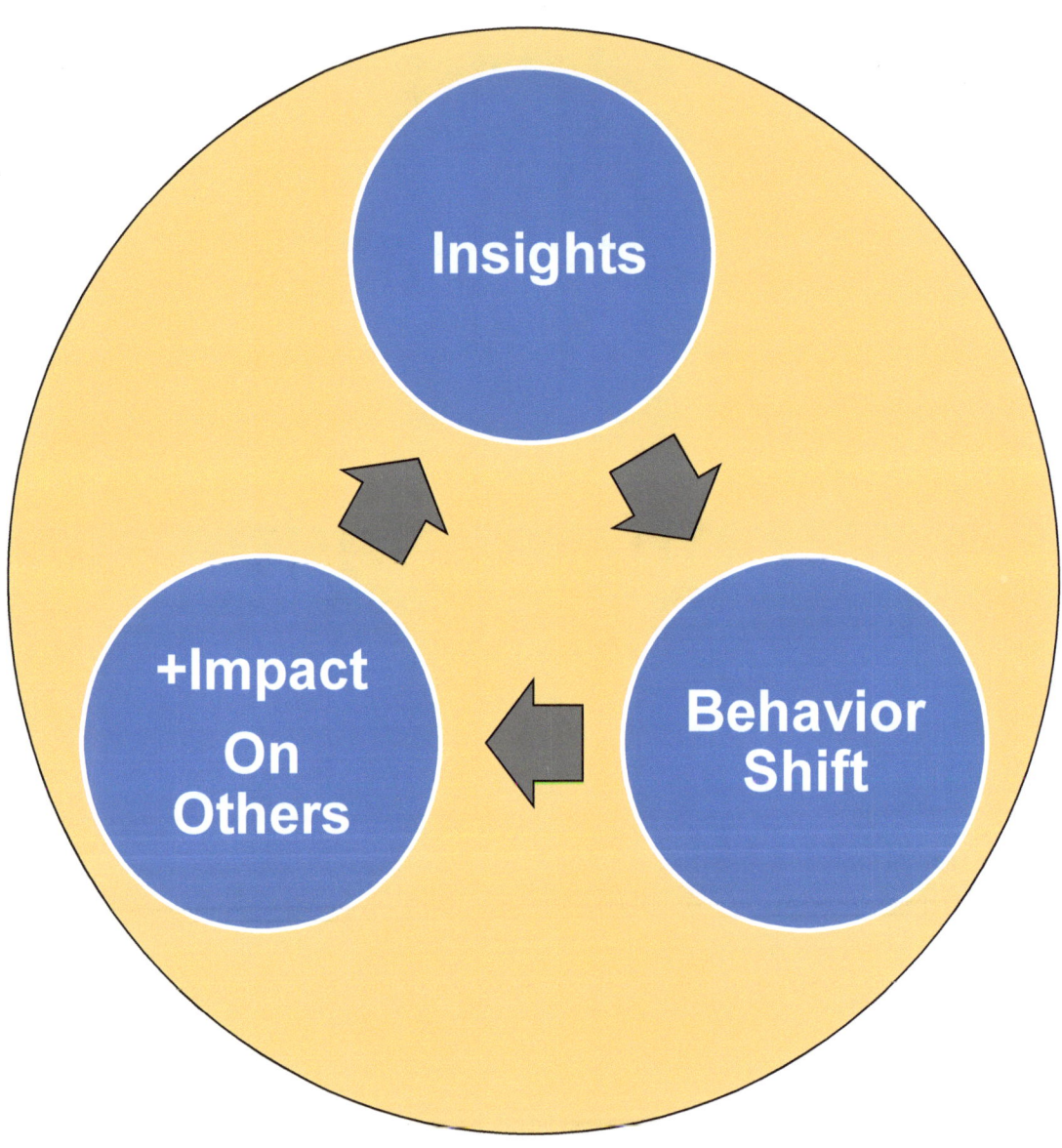

1. **Customer Focus Culture**

2. **Your Brand,**
   Your Reputation

3. **Customer Map & Plan**

Customer Focus

Customer Focus

Enhanced Results

Support accountability

Create and maintain alignment

Build trust – Walk-the-talk

WIIFM

What's in it for you?

Customer Focus Culture

External customers are companies or individuals who uses your company's products or services but is not part of your organization. External customers contact your company to buy your products or services

Internal customers are all the members of your organization

Everyone in their unique way requires assistance from each other to fulfill his/her job duties

Each person is your customer and you are their customer

Those who have direct contact with our external customers represent the customer to our company.

Whether you have direct contact with our external customers or not, each of us has a connection to the external customer through the people we work with.

Each person represents the voice of the customer in all of our interactions.

Check Your Attitude®

Sb Sabotage									**Sv** Service

Vt Victim	**Re** Resigned	**Df** Defensive	**En** Envious	**Sp** Suspicious	**Tr** Trusting	**Cr** Creative	**In** Inspired	**Cm** Committed	**Vi** Visionary
Ad Adversary	**Bl** Blaming	**Sr** Sarcastic	**Ag** Angry	**Fs** Frustrated	**Eg** Engaged	**Pa** Passionate	**Hu** Humorous	**Ac** Accountable	**Av** Activator
Rs Rescuer	**Su** Superior	**Cn** Controlling	**Ha** Hidden Agenda	**Ar** Arrogant	**Ap** Accepting	**Tp** Transparent	**Cf** Confident	**Hm** Humble	**Co** Coach
Sk Skeptic	**Cy** Cynical	**Ct** Critical	**Is** Insulted	**Jg** Judgmental	**Cu** Curious	**Ob** Objective	**Sp** Supportive	**Md** Mindful	**Mn** Mentor

Negative Spin   **Choice**   **Positive Spin**

Interactive web site: www.checkyourtude.com

When you are the customer, how do you like to be approached?

Circle at least 1 for each row

 14

5th Owner

4th On Board

3rd Bobble Head

2nd On a position

1st Out of the game

When you are the customer, how do you like to be approached?

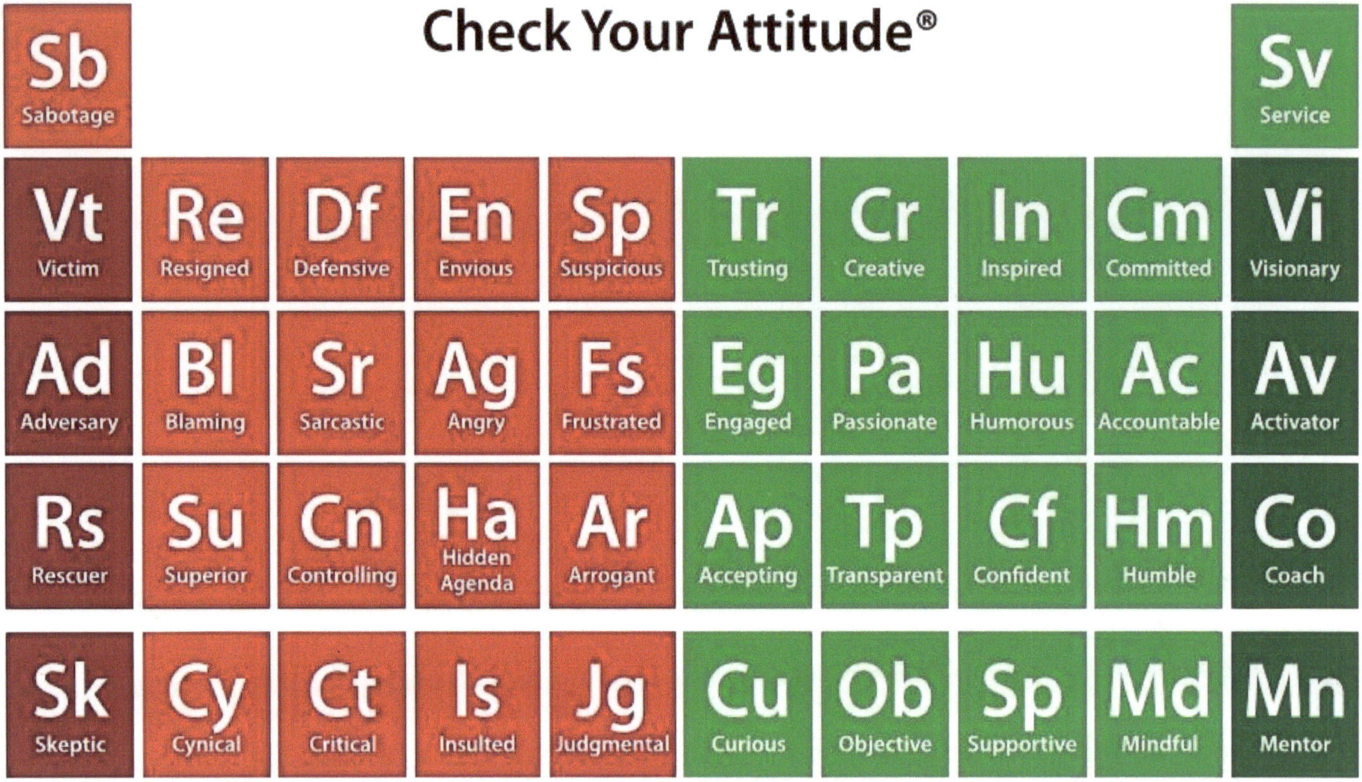

Check Your Attitude®

Sb Sabotage									**Sv** Service

Vt Victim	**Re** Resigned	**Df** Defensive	**En** Envious	**Sp** Suspicious	**Tr** Trusting	**Cr** Creative	**In** Inspired	**Cm** Committed	**Vi** Visionary
Ad Adversary	**Bl** Blaming	**Sr** Sarcastic	**Ag** Angry	**Fs** Frustrated	**Eg** Engaged	**Pa** Passionate	**Hu** Humorous	**Ac** Accountable	**Av** Activator
Rs Rescuer	**Su** Superior	**Cn** Controlling	**Ha** Hidden Agenda	**Ar** Arrogant	**Ap** Accepting	**Tp** Transparent	**Cf** Confident	**Hm** Humble	**Co** Coach
Sk Skeptic	**Cy** Cynical	**Ct** Critical	**Is** Insulted	**Jg** Judgmental	**Cu** Curious	**Ob** Objective	**Sp** Supportive	**Md** Mindful	**Mn** Mentor

Negative Spin   **Choice**   **Positive Spin**

Interactive web site: www.checkyourtude.com

How do you tend to approach the employees that you work with?

When under stress how do you approach the people you work with?

 16

How do you tend to approach the people that you work with?

When under stress?

The core business of any corporation is to create increasing value for its customers.

Value gets created in the interface between each employee and the employees and their customers.

Since it is expected for you to create increasing value, your job regardless of your title is to inspire, encourage, and support everyone in their work.

Leadership or Drama

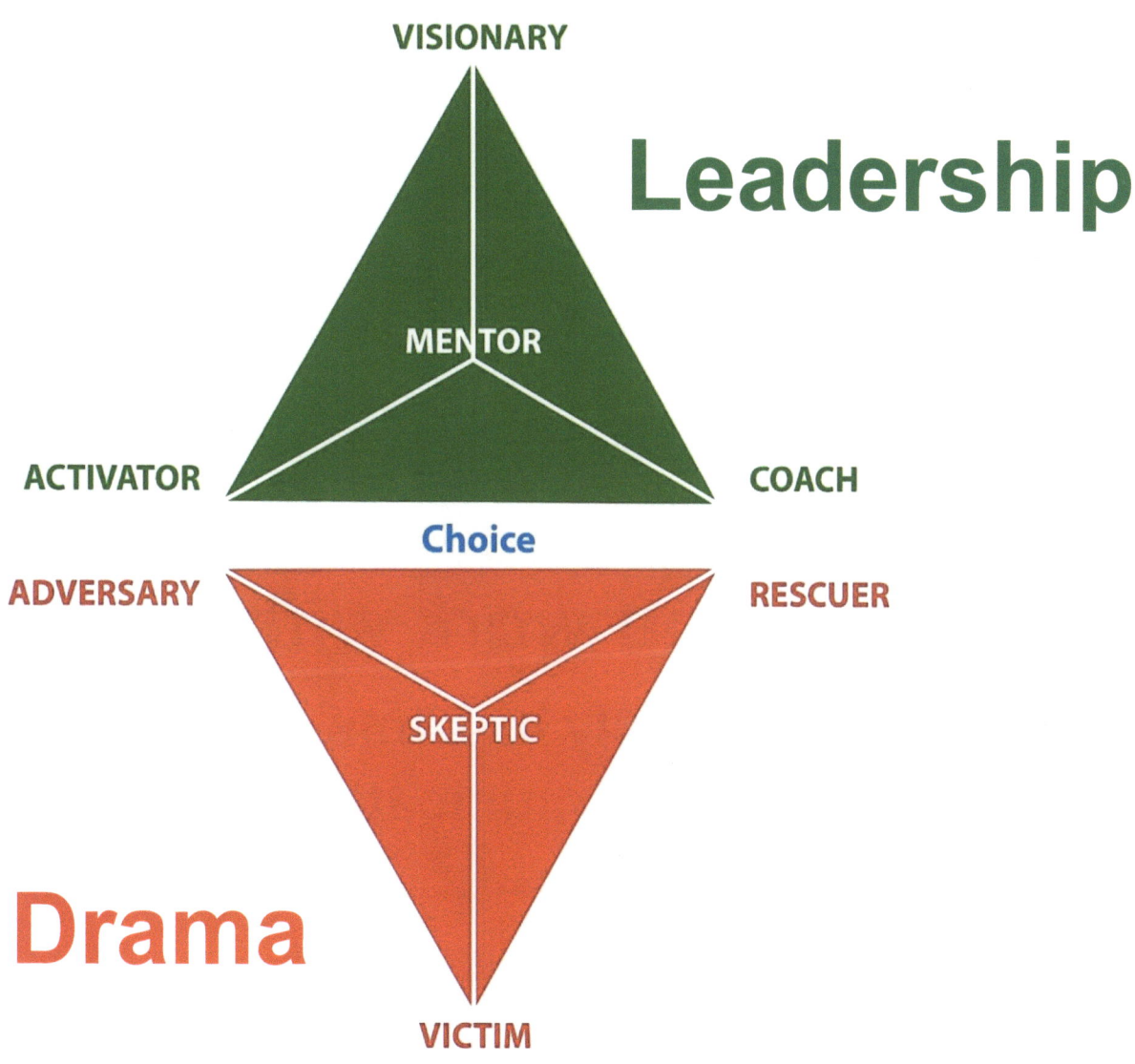

What does it mean to you to treat all employees as your customer?

How do you need to different in how you interact with the people you work with?

Especially in terms of the quality of your communications & your attitude?

The first step in exceeding your customer's expectations is to know those expectations.

Roy H. Williams

 23

What is your Brand?

Define what your brand stands for, its core values and tone of voice, and then communicate consistently in those terms.

Simon Mainwaring

 25

Your brand

Your brand is represented by the first thoughts that people have when they think about you. It is your *reputation*

The quality of work that you do AND the experience people have of working with you are key components of your brand

Your brand represents the value you bring to the business

Create your brand

1. Establish your core values

2. Become your best

3. Be approachable

4. Speak positively about others

5. Be of service to others

1. Establish your values

Your values are what motivate you at the deepest level

Your values are what you stand for, what you believe in, and what you want to live up to

Your values guide your thinking, feeling and acting

What are your top 3 values?

2. Become your best

Every good brand involves the notion of expertise. Nike brands itself as an expert in creating quality and fashionable sportswear.

If you have stopped learning and challenging yourself, find a new area to grow in.

Keep developing your expertise and growing professionally. Continue learning and updating your knowledge.

How are you investing in being your best?

3. Be approachable

You need to think hard about HOW you act
People should easily feel like they want to
work with you

Get plenty of ongoing feedback from those
you work with on you can improve your
working relationship. It may be humbling at
first but soon you will gain a deeper
confidence from the input you receive

What is the experience you want people to have when they interact with you?

4. Speak positively about others

Spread the word about the strengths of others and their good work

Ironically your credibility goes up when you speak positively about others

Create a positive reputation for those you work with rather than negative gossip

What are the positive stories you can tell about others?

5. Be of service

It is simple - put others first, the rest will take care of itself.

A person who is serving others at work is automatically valuable.

Operate from your unique blend of leadership strengths:
Visionary, Activator, Coach, Mentor

How will you be of service to all those around you?

Great companies that build an enduring brand have an emotional relationship with customers that has no barrier.

And that emotional relationship is on the most important characteristic, which is trust.

Howard Schultz

Customer Map

At a glance you will see all of your important relationships

Your map helps to keep you on track to extraordinary results

Customer Map

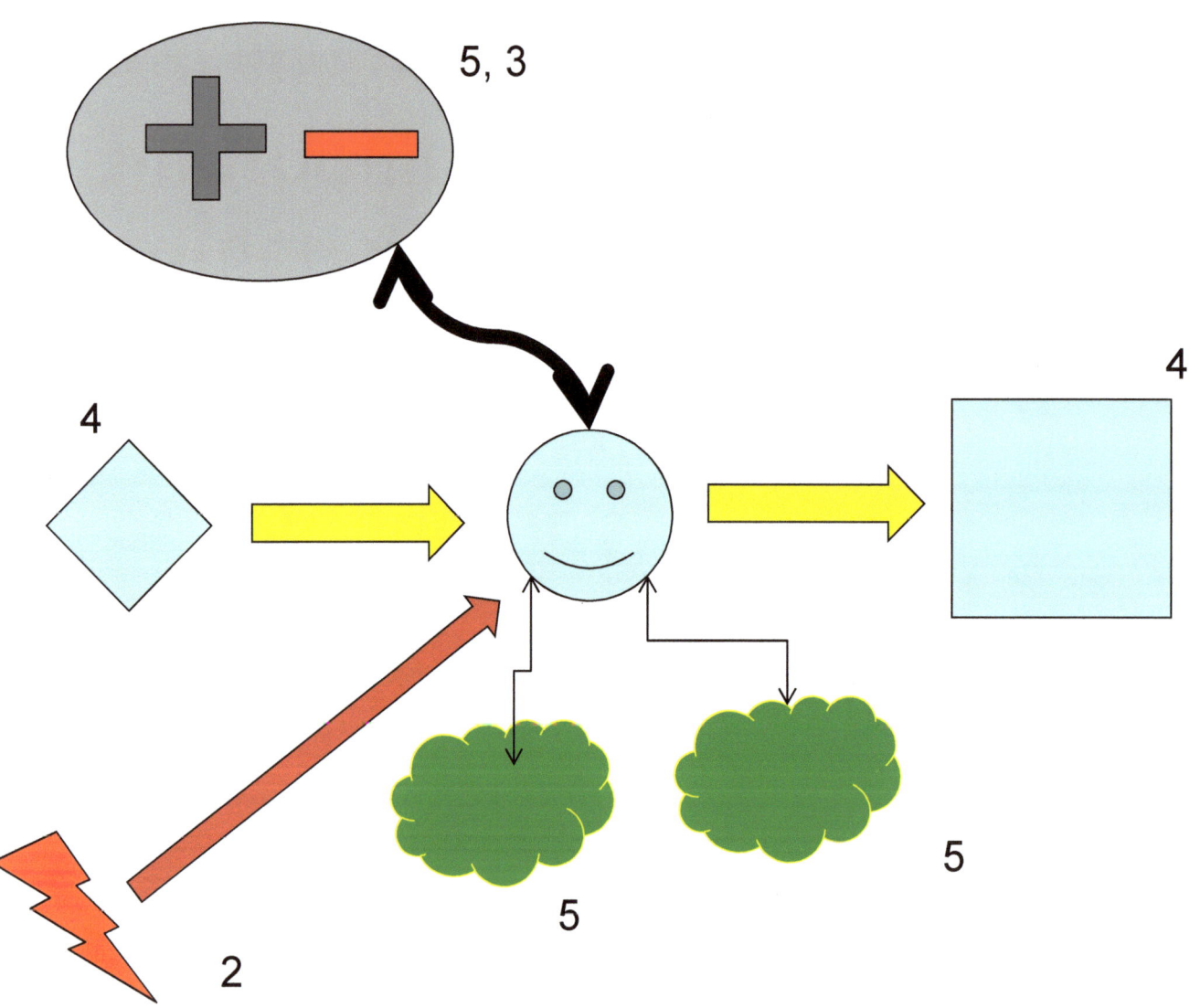

Customer Map

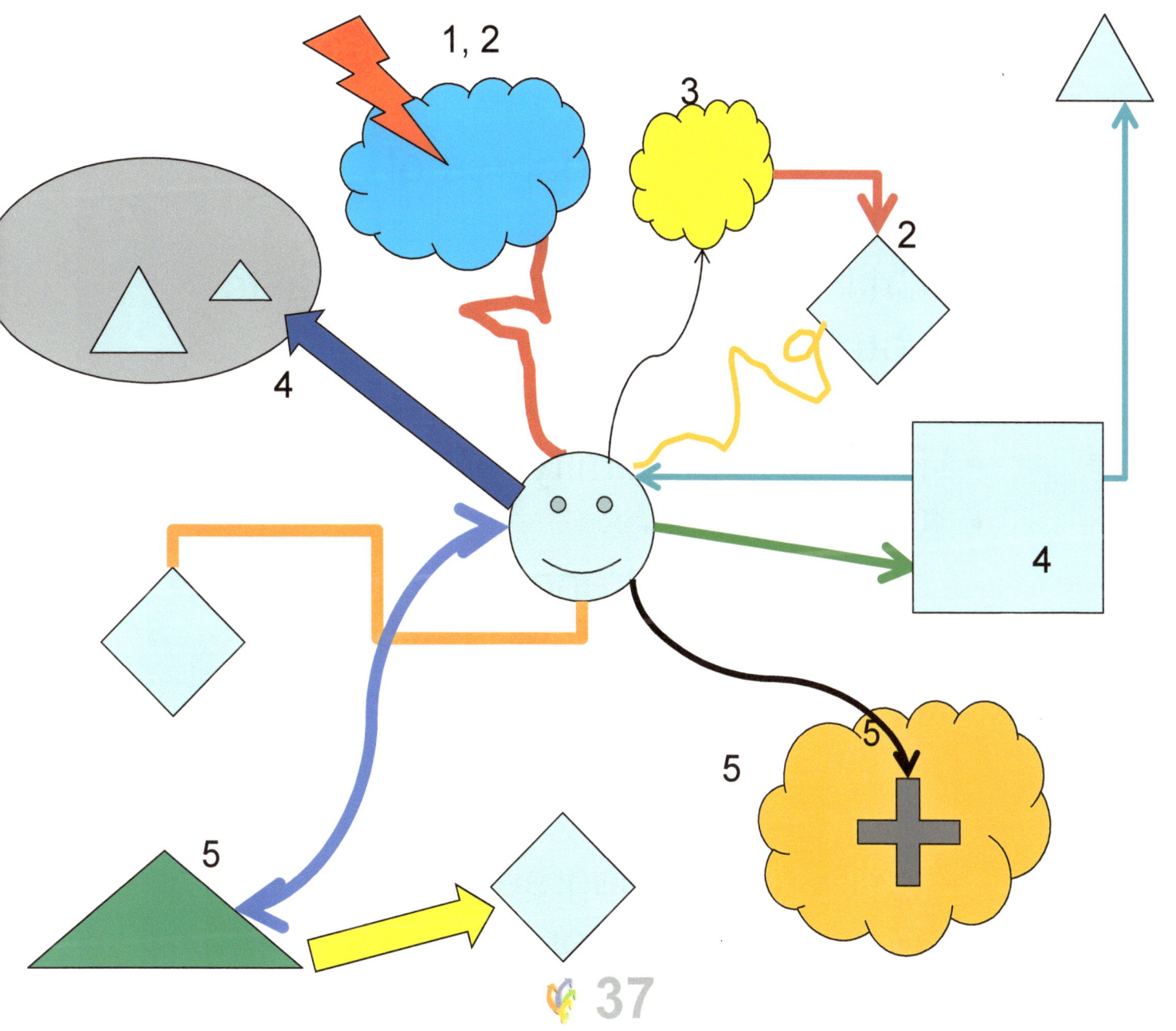

Customer Map Key

Key – Show relationships – people, functions, groups
- Size & Shape – degree of influence, impact
- Critical path – Who is essential to your work
- Dependencies – who you rely on
- Position - proximity
- Connector lines
    - Quality & strength of the connection/relationship
    - Direct & indirect relationships
    - Arrows – flow of direction, information, etc.
- Indicate your degree of alignment for each person or group (1-5)

Customer Map

What are you learning about your internal customer relationships?

What can you do to improve your relationships?

Customer Plan

Customer In vs. Product Out

Customer In =
Proactive
Engagement

Customer In

STEP 1: DEFINE & ALIGN EXPECTATIONS

STEP 4: REVIEW & VALIDATE

STEP 2: MAINTAIN COMMUNICATION

STEP 3: BE ACCOUNTABLE

Customer In - Step 1

STEP 1: DEFINE & ALIGN EXPECTATIONS

- Use the Conversation Cycle to define clear deliverable and timelines
- Document expectations

Customer In - Step 1

**STEP 1:
DEFINE &
ALIGN
EXPECTATIONS**

- What is the end result/deliverable?
- What are the key inputs?
- When will you deliver?

Customer In - Step 2

**STEP 2:
MAINTAIN
COMMUNICATION**

- Have frequent ongoing 2-way updates
- Don't wait for things to go wrong.
- Be transparent with challenges as they arise & invite others to solve problems with you
- Respond quickly to requests

Customer In - Step 2

STEP 2:
MAINTAIN
COMMUNICATION

- This is the progress I am making
- These are the challenges and the plan to meet them
- I will be on time (or when)

- How is the work going on…?
- How can I support you?

Customer In - Step 3

STEP 3:
BE
ACCOUNTABLE

"It's better to fall on your sword, than get stabbed in the back."
Jim Peal

Customer In - Step 3

STEP 3:
BE
ACCOUNTABLE

Meeting Rules of Engagement

1. Speak about the solution you are seeking vs. who you think is at fault
2. Ask, "What is another way to say that?" as a way to coach others into the green in meetings
3. Call an "**Attitude Check**" time-out when things and emotions go into the red. Pause 90 seconds to cool down

Customer In - Step 3

STEP 3:
BE
ACCOUNTABLE

Clean-Up

Engage in clean up as soon as you are aware that there has been negative impact on the other. Don't wait.

1. Take full accountability for what you did or didn't do and for the consequences
2. Apologize. Let the other person know that you are sorry about how they were impacted – no excuses
3. Make a promise about your future action with regard to keeping your commitment

Supporting Accountability

Get into positive mindset

1. Frame the conversation

   "I'd like to talk with you about your deliverables for this project.

2. Share and compare the data and perceptions

   "It seems like you are having some challenges, how is are things going from your point of view?"

   "We had agreed this would be completed by _____ and now this is the impact it is having____.

3. Create an aligned understanding

   "Is there anything we are missing to get on the same page for where we are today?"

4. Create the plan to move forward

   "What do we/you need to do to get things back on track?"

5. Thank them and set up follow-up

   "Thanks for this conversation. Let's meet every _____ to see how we are progressing"

Customer In – Step 4

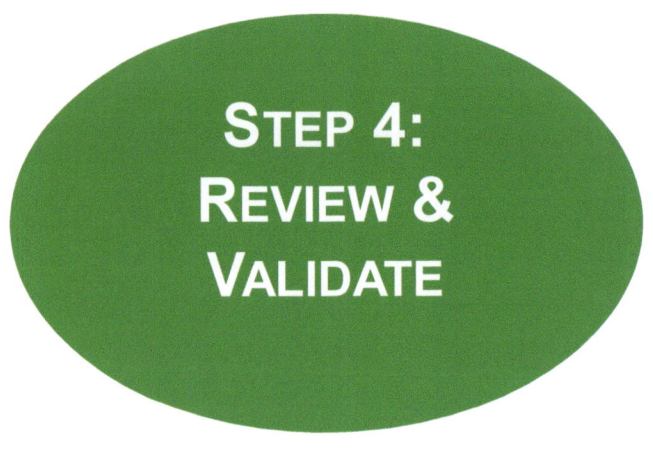

STEP 4:
REVIEW &
VALIDATE

Debrief

1. What worked especially well?
2. What aspects did not work?
3. What areas needed more support?
4. How could we better prepare for the "surprise factor?"
5. How will we apply what we have learned?

Customer In – Step 4

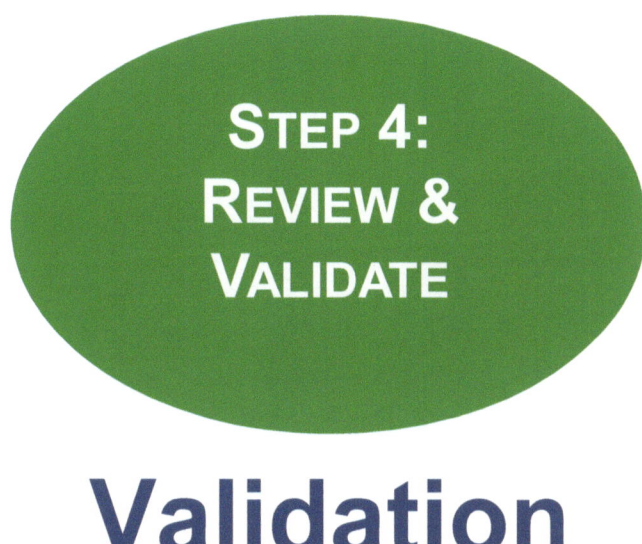

STEP 4:
REVIEW &
VALIDATE

Validation

1. **Be Authentic**

2. **Be Specific**

3. **Be Personal**

4. **Be Futuristic**

Say "Thank You." to receive the validation

53

Customer In

STEP 1:
DEFINE & ALIGN
EXPECTATIONS

STEP 4:
REVIEW &
VALIDATE

STEP 2:
MAINTAIN
COMMUNICATION

STEP 3:
BE
ACCOUNTABLE

**Debrief:
Look at your customer
map and see where
you can apply the
Customer In steps to
improve your
relationships**

Session Take-Aways

- Key Insights

- Behavior changes

- Expected Positive Impact

Next Steps

1. Review your map and discuss your plan with your manager/supervisor.

2. Discuss how you would like to develop yourself to be your best.

Jim Peal, Ph.D.

Books and Kindle on Amazon:
Daring to Have Real Conversations in Business
Check Your Attitude at the Door
Leading Change
Executive Influence
Culture Change Series

See Jim on TEDx Talks – *"Decisions That Define Us"*
Google Jim Peal TED talk

Jim provides Executive, Team and Organizational
Coaching & Consulting

Tel. (01) 805-966-3323

www.leadershipDG.com

www.checkyourtude.com

 58

www.ingramcontent.com/pod-product-compliance
Lightning Source LLC
Chambersburg PA
CBHW050802180526
45159CB00004B/1525